Made in the Wild: Animal Builders

Robert Norris

Educational Media

rourkeeducationalmedia.com

Scan for Related Titles
and Teacher Resources

Teaching Focus:
Fluency: Using Expression - Have students read aloud to practice reading with expression and with appropriate pacing.

Before Reading:

Building Academic Vocabulary and Background Knowledge
Before reading a book, it is important to set the stage for your child or student by using pre-reading strategies. This will help them develop their vocabulary, increase their reading comprehension, and make connections across the curriculum.

1. *Read the title and look at the cover. Let's make predictions about what this book will be about.*
2. *Take a picture walk by talking about the pictures/photographs in the book. Implant the vocabulary as you take the picture walk. Be sure to talk about the text features such as headings, Table of Contents, glossary, bolded words, captions, charts/ diagrams, or Index.*
3. Have students read the first page of text with you then have students read the remaining text.
4. *Strategy Talk – use to assist students while reading.*
   - *Get your mouth ready*
   - *Look at the picture*
   - *Think…does it make sense*
   - *Think…does it look right*
   - *Think…does it sound right*
   - *Chunk it – by looking for a part you know*
5. *Read it again.*
6. *After reading the book complete the activities below.*

Content Area Vocabulary
Use glossary words in a sentence.

colony
construct
master
mound
queen
reefs

After Reading:

Comprehension and Extension Activity
After reading the book, work on the following questions with your child or students in order to check their level of reading comprehension and content mastery.

1. *What does construct mean? (Summarize)*
2. *Why do animals build? (Summarize)*
3. *Why do some animals share the same home? (Asking questions)*
4. *What do bees build? (Summarize)*

Extension Activity
Now it's time for you to be an animal builder! Choose one of the animals from the book. Using various art supplies, construct the animal's home. Make sure you label your picture or model. Write a caption for your picture or model that explains the purpose and importance of this home for your animal.

Stack the blocks. Make it tall, make it wide.
Build it up. Who goes inside?

Animals That Build

Humans are not the only ones that build things. Some animals are great builders. The things they build help them survive in the wild.

Crab Homes

African Weaver Nest

Stork Nest

Animals build to keep safe and warm. Some build places to live together. They build to protect their babies. Some even build to catch food.

Sociable Weaver Nest

Knock, knock. The sociable weaver nest is like a hotel for birds. Weavers stay there together as a group. They let other birds stay there, too.

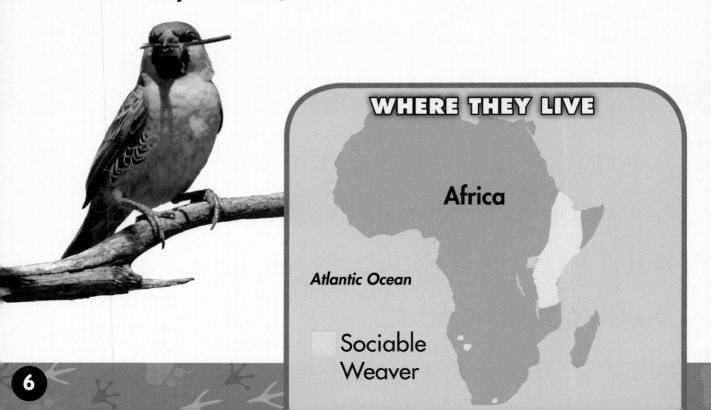

WHERE THEY LIVE

Africa

Atlantic Ocean

Sociable Weaver

The sociable weaver needs a place to stay safe. It builds a nest.

Sociable Weaver Nest

Weavers let other birds stay in their nests because more birds means more eyes watching for predators.

Termite Mound

Up and up, the termite **mound** rises from the ground. It is made of dirt, the termites' spit, and even their poop!

Termite Mound

8

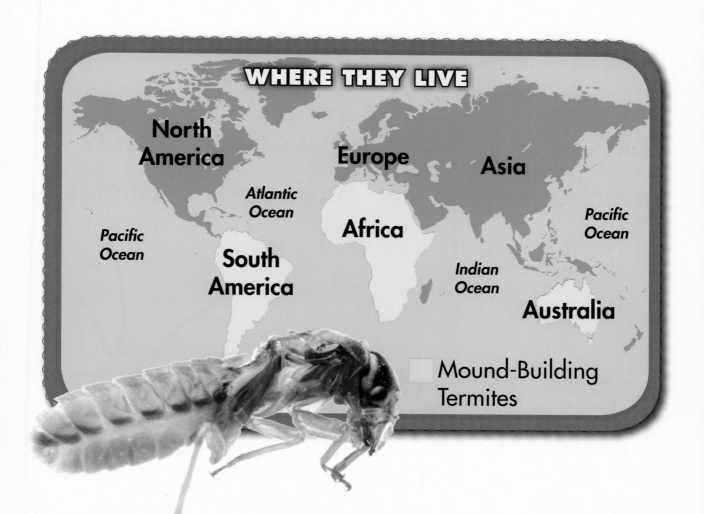

WHERE THEY LIVE

North America

Atlantic Ocean

Pacific Ocean

South America

Europe

Africa

Asia

Pacific Ocean

Indian Ocean

Australia

Mound-Building Termites

The termites need a place to live together. They build a mound.

Spider Web

The spider is a **master** weaver. Its web stretches across tree branches. It catches its next meal in the sticky web.

WHERE THEY LIVE

North America

Europe

Asia

Atlantic Ocean

Africa

Pacific Ocean

Pacific Ocean

South America

Indian Ocean

Australia

Spiders

The spider needs to catch its food. It builds a web.

Spider Web

Coral Reef

Coral **reefs** are so big, some can be seen from space! Corals make ocean reefs as they grow. The reefs give younger corals a place to live.

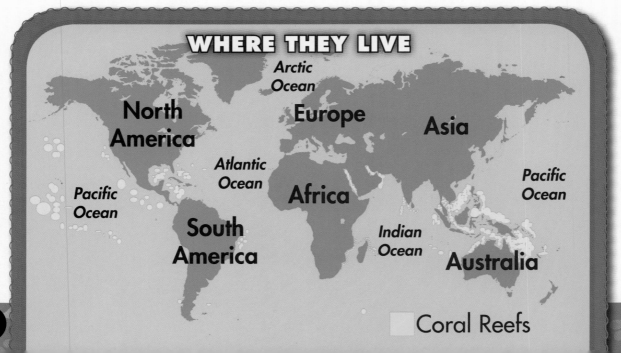

WHERE THEY LIVE

Arctic Ocean

North America

Europe

Asia

Atlantic Ocean

Pacific Ocean

Africa

Pacific Ocean

South America

Indian Ocean

Australia

Coral Reefs

The coral need a place to live.
They build a reef.

Coral

Coral reefs are home to about 25 percent of all ocean life.

Beaver Dam

Mud, logs, sticks, and rocks are used to **construct** a beaver dam. The dam turns streams into ponds. The ponds are safe places for beavers to live and build their homes.

WHERE THEY LIVE

North America

Pacific Ocean

Atlantic Ocean

Beavers

The beavers need a place to stay safe.
They build a dam.

Beaver Dam

Ant Colony

Tiny ants do big work. Together they dig a great **colony**. The **queen** lays her eggs underground. Some colonies are home to millions of ants.

Only the opening to the ant colony is visible above ground. The colony's huge system of tunnels and chambers are hidden underground.

Ant Hill

The ants need a safe place to have their babies. They build a colony.

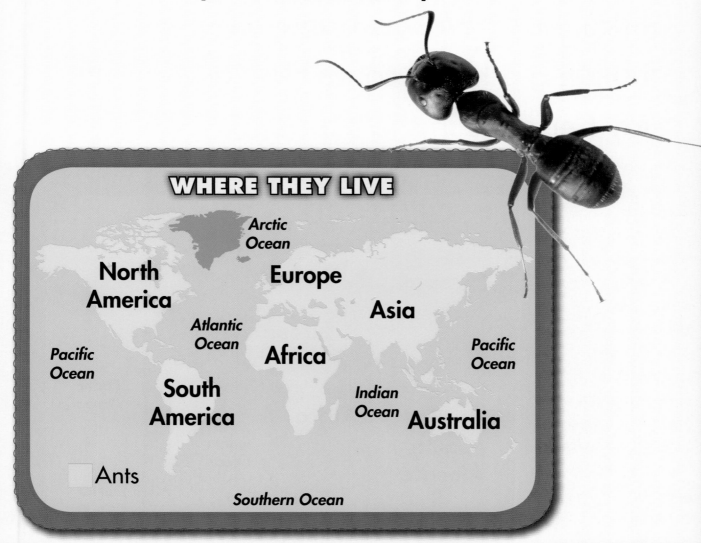

WHERE THEY LIVE

Arctic Ocean

North America

Europe

Asia

Pacific Ocean

Atlantic Ocean

Africa

Pacific Ocean

South America

Indian Ocean

Australia

Ants

Southern Ocean

Honeycomb

Buzz. Buzz. Worker honeybees are building a honeycomb. The queen will lay her eggs in the spaces.

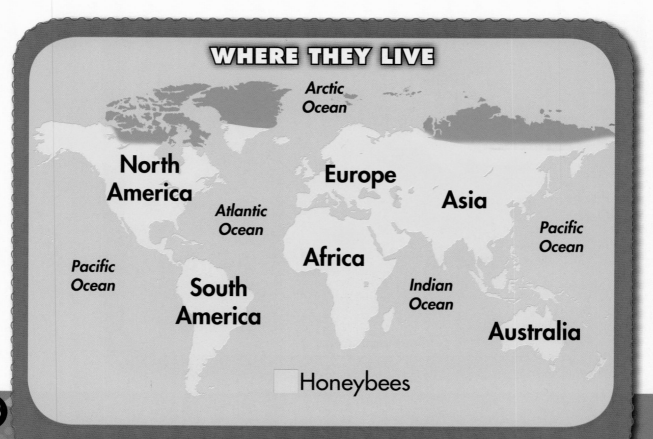

WHERE THEY LIVE

Arctic Ocean

North America

Europe

Asia

Atlantic Ocean

Pacific Ocean

Pacific Ocean

Africa

South America

Indian Ocean

Australia

Honeybees

Honeycomb

The bees need a place to raise their young and store food. They build a honeycomb.

Cliff Swallow Nest

High in the air, on the sides of cliffs and rocks, the cliff swallow makes its mud nest. The mud nest dries hard. It keeps the swallow and its babies safe.

The swallow needs safety. It builds a nest.

WHERE THEY LIVE

North America

Atlantic Ocean

Pacific Ocean

South America

Cliff Swallow

When animals build, they make unique structures that help them survive in the wild.

Cliff Swallow

Cliff Swallow Nest

Photo Glossary

 **colony** (KAH-luh-nee): A colony is a place where a group of animals lives together.

 **construct** (kuhn-STRUHKT): Construct is another word for build.

 **master** (MAS-tur): When you have mastered a skill, you are able to perform it very well.

mound (mound): A mound is a large pile that may contain dirt, sand, rock, and other materials.

queen (kween): In an insect colony, the queen is the female insect that lays eggs.

reefs (reefs): Reefs are underwater chains of rock and sand that are home to many ocean plants and animals.

Index

About the Author

Robert Norris writes books, articles, and essays on science topics for young people. He lives with his family in New York. Robert has seen many animal buildings up close, and hopes that one day he can see a sociable weaver nest.

Meet The Author!
www.meetREMauthors.com

Websites

pbskids.org/zoom/activities/sci/buildadam.html

kids.nationalgeographic.com/kids/photos/coral-reef

kids.nationalgeographic.com/kids/photos/gallery/spider-webs

www.rourkeeducationalmedia.com

PHOTO CREDITS: Cover: © Khlongwangchao; title page: © Noluma; page 3: © vectorlib.com; page 4: © zanskar, © SuperC; page 5: © agitons; © Alta Oosthuizen; page 7: © Nico Smit; page 8, 23: © twildlife; page 9: © defun; page 10: © Smitt; page 11, 22: © JanetLa; page 13, 23: © Tetyana Kochneva; page 15, 22: © sstevens3, © Jill Chen; page 16, 22: © knape; page 17: stocksnapp; page 19: © AlexStar; page 21: © Frank Leung, © opel_ru; page 23 (middle): ©skynetphoto

Edited by: Jill Sherman
Cover design by: Jen Thompson
Interior design by: Rhea Magaro

Library of Congress PCN Data

Made in the Wild: Animal Buiders/ Robert Norris
(Close Up on Amazing Animals)
ISBN (hard cover)(alk. paper) 978-1-62717-634-7
ISBN (soft cover) 978-1-62717-756-6
ISBN (e-Book) 978-1-62717-877-8
Library of Congress Control Number: 2014934202
Printed in the United States of America, North Mankato, Minnesota